1/07

79 Decorative Alphabets

for Designers and Craftspeople

Edited by
Carol Belanger Grafton

DOVER PUBLICATIONS, INC.
Mineola, New York

Bibliographical Note

79 Decorative Alphabets for Designers and Craftspeople was originally published by Dover Publications, Inc., in 1981 as *Decorative Alphabets for Needleworkers, Craftsmen and Artists.* The various sources for the illustrations are indicated in the Publisher's Note.

Library of Congress Cataloging-in-Publication Data

Grafton, Carol Belanger.
[Decorative alphabets for needleworkers, craftsmen & artists]
79 decorative alphabets for designers and craftspeople / edited by Carol Belanger Grafton.
p. cm. — (Dover pictorial archive series)
Originally published in 1981 as Decorative alphabets for needleworkers, craftsmen and artists.
ISBN 0-486-41715-8 (pbk.)
1. Alphabets—Specimens. 2. Decoration and ornament. I. Title: Seventy-nine decorative alphabets for designers and craftspeople. II. Title. III. Series.

NK3630 .G7 2001
745.6'1—dc21

00-052365

Manufactured in the United States of America
Dover Publications, Inc., 31 East 2nd Street, Mineola, N.Y. 11501

PUBLISHER'S NOTE

The history of decorative alphabets began with the ornamentation of handwritten and, later, printed books, in which decorative letters played an integral part as the initial letters of chapters, paragraphs and headings, with the largest letters making the most important textual divisions. Although printers and book designers no longer make extensive use of decorative letters, letters of this kind are still effectively employed to create striking advertisements and cover designs. In media other than printing, however, the use of decorative letters is increasing, and it is principally for the creative needleworker, craftsman and artist, whose applications of decorative alphabets are limited only by the imagination, that this volume is intended.

Graphic designer Carol Belanger Grafton has gathered over two thousand letters, including seventy-nine complete alphabets, many from rare sources that have long been out of print, and all copyright free. The volume also reflects the keen eye of Dover Publications' former needlecraft specialist, Rita Weiss, who participated in the final selection. Needleworkers may wish to make use of any number of lacy, elegant shapes (see, for example, pages 4, 6 and 7); some of the letter designs included were originally created as transfer patterns. But they will also find many styles ideally suited for needlepoint, embroidery, cross stitch and latch hooking that were first conceived for other purposes. Woodcraftsmen may choose to carve, or burn in with an electric pen, the dot letters on page 11 or the bolder shapes found on page 34. Some of the ex-tremely elaborate alphabets, like the one beginning on page 81, will inspire artists interested in the free play of abstract shapes.

Most of the letters and alphabets in this volume were derived from the following sources:

Alphabets, Monograms, Initials, & Crests. New York: F. W. Bullinger, n.d.

Artistic Alphabets for Marking and Engrossing. New York: Butterick, 1897.

Bergling, J. M. *Art Monograms and Lettering for the Use of Engravers, Artists, Designers, and Art Workmen.* Chicago: J. M. Bergling, 1914.

Brown, Frank Chouteau. *Letters & Lettering: A Treatise with 200 Examples.* Boston: Bates & Guild, 1921.

Delamotte, F. *The Book of Ornamental Alphabets, Ancient and Mediaeval, from the Eighth Century, with Numerals.* London: C. Prang, 1916.

Esser, Hermann. *Draughtsman's Alphabets.* New York: Keuffer and Esser, 1877.

Henderson's Sign Painter. Newark, N.J.: R. Henderson, 1906.

Hollister, Paul. *American Alphabets.* New York, 1930.

Lindegren, Erik. *ABC of Lettering and Printing Types*, Vol. B. New York: Museum Books, 1960.

The Real Pen-Work Self-Instructor in Penmanship. Pittsfield, Mass.: Knowles & Maxim, 1881.

Stevens, Thomas Wood. *Lettering.* New York: Prang, 1916.

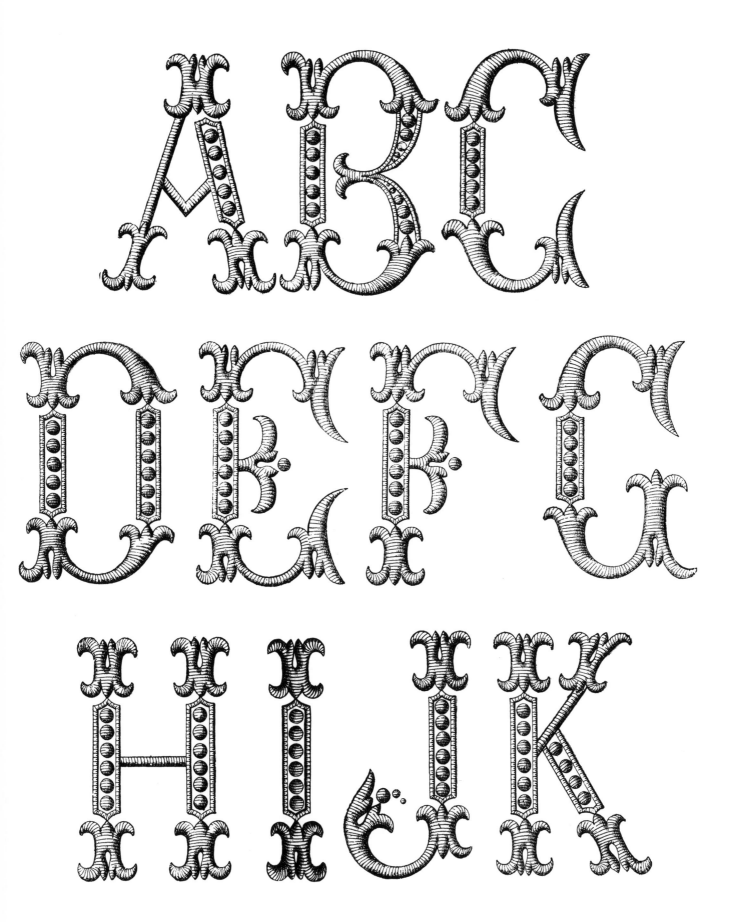

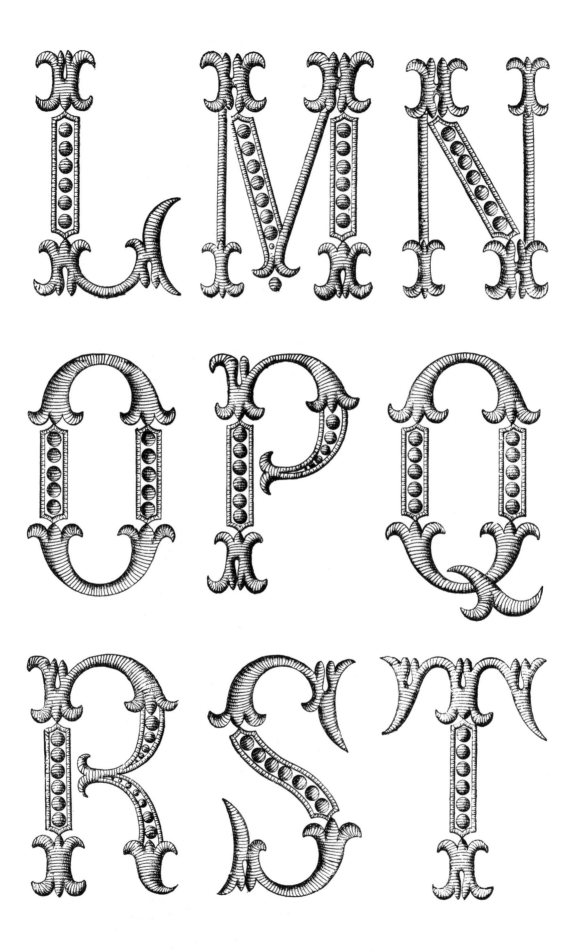

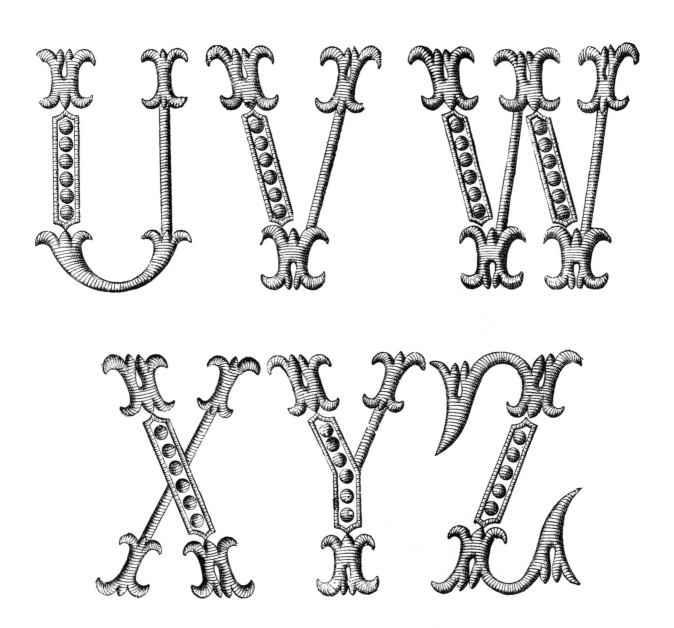

A B C
D E F G H
I K L M N O
P Q R S T U V
W X Y Z

A B C
D E F G H
I K L M N O
P Q R S T U V
W X Y Z

A B
C D E F
G H I K
L M N O P
Q R S
T U V W
X Y Z

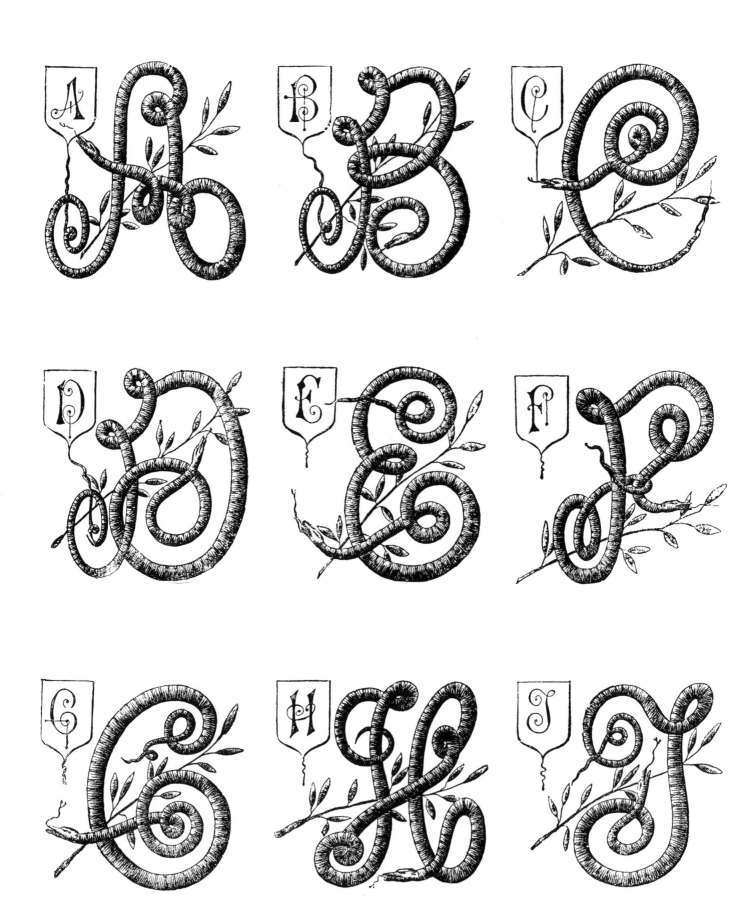

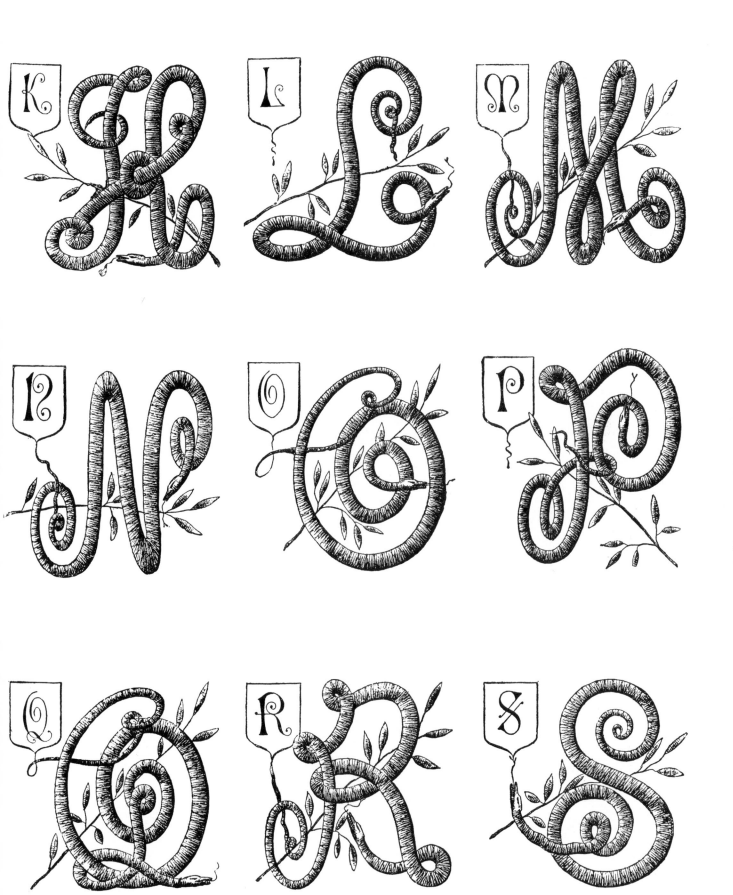

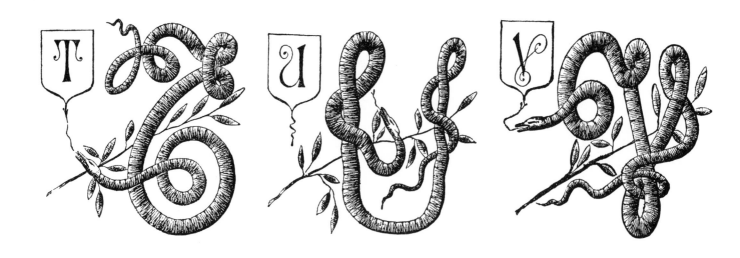

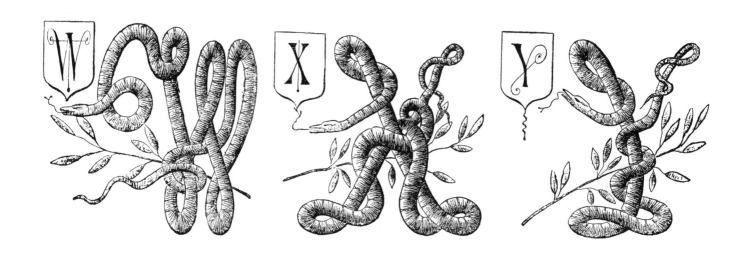

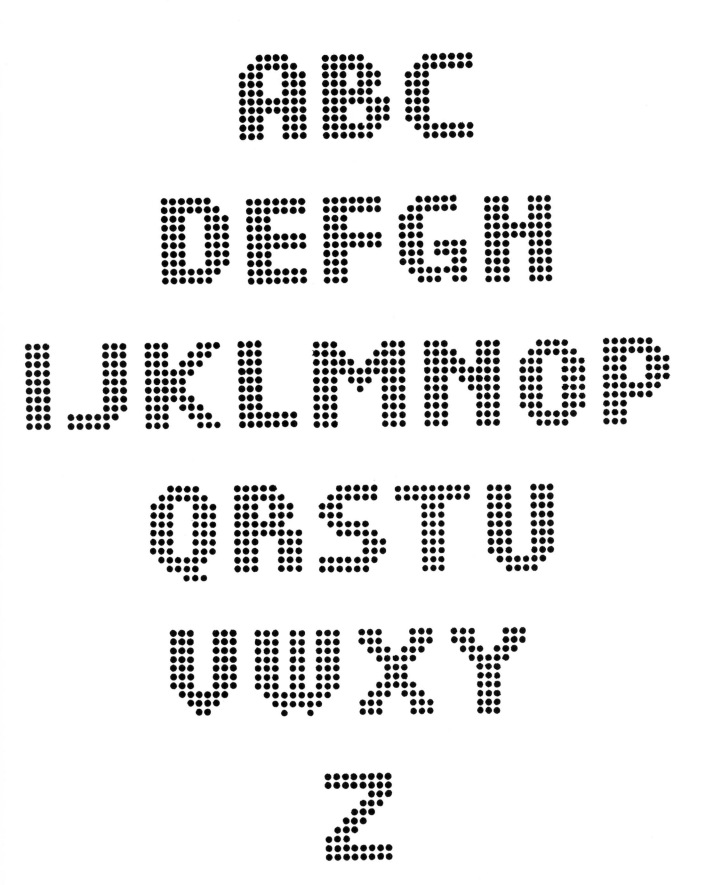

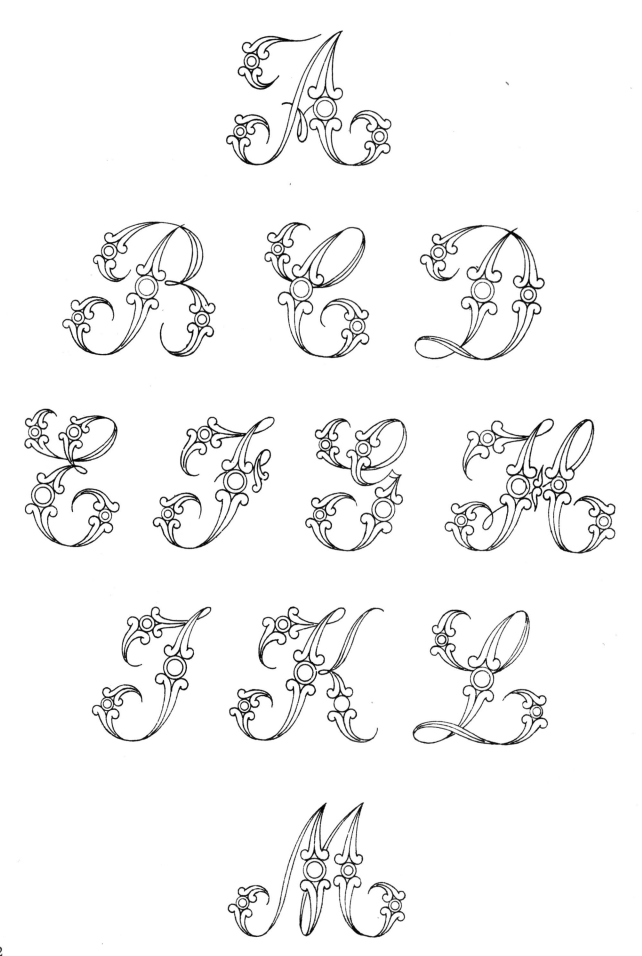

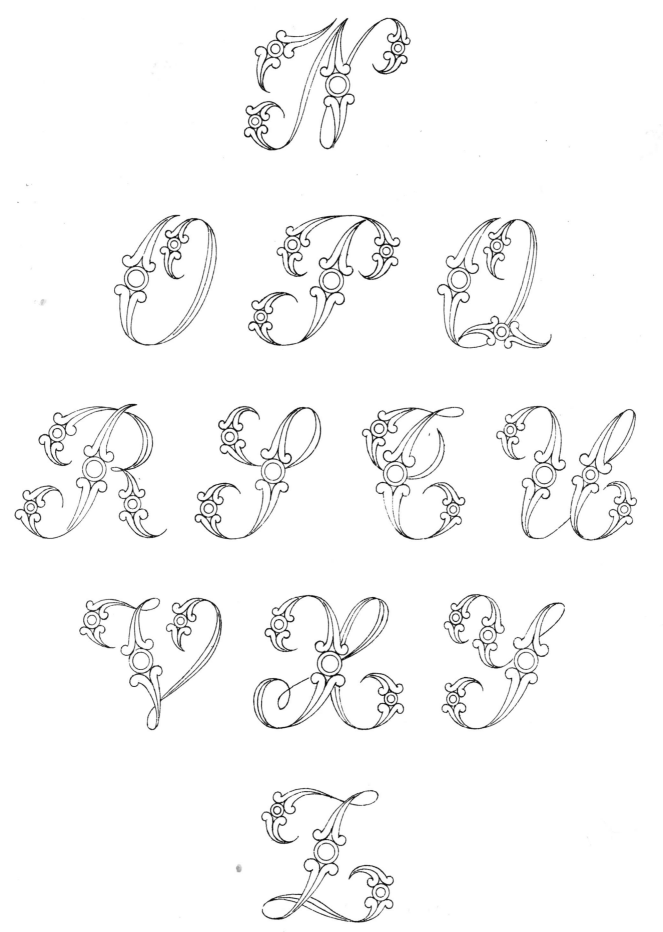

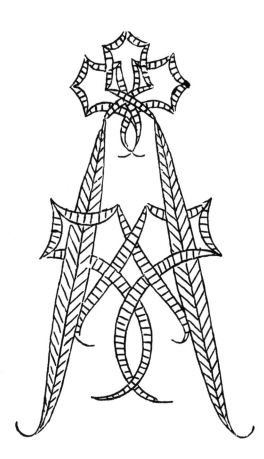

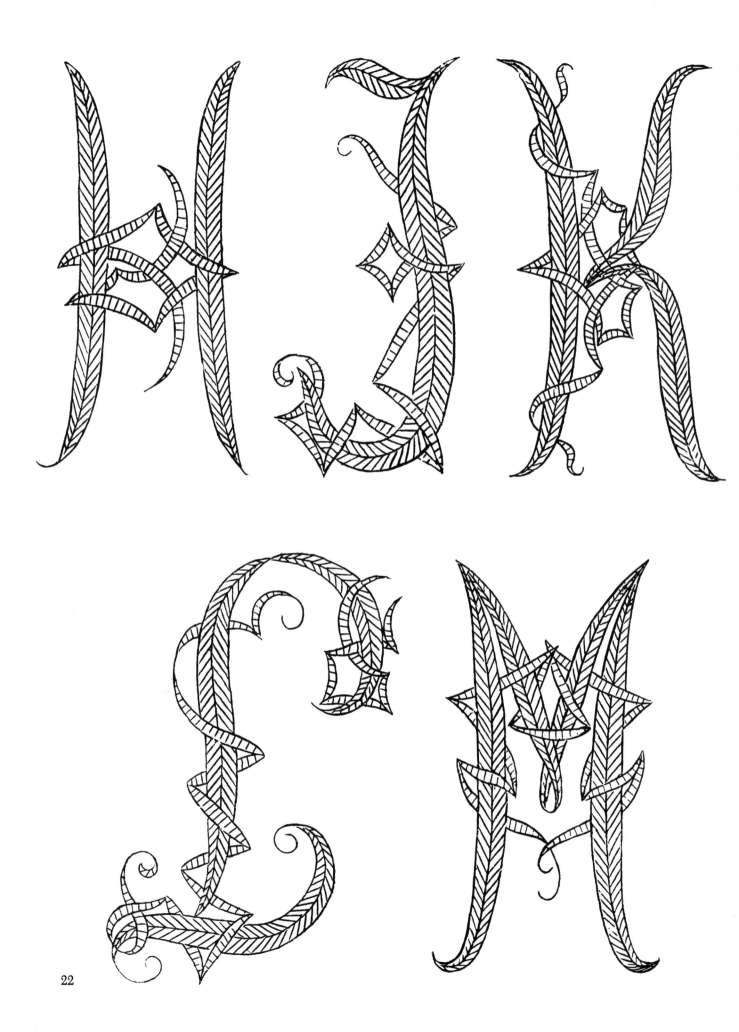

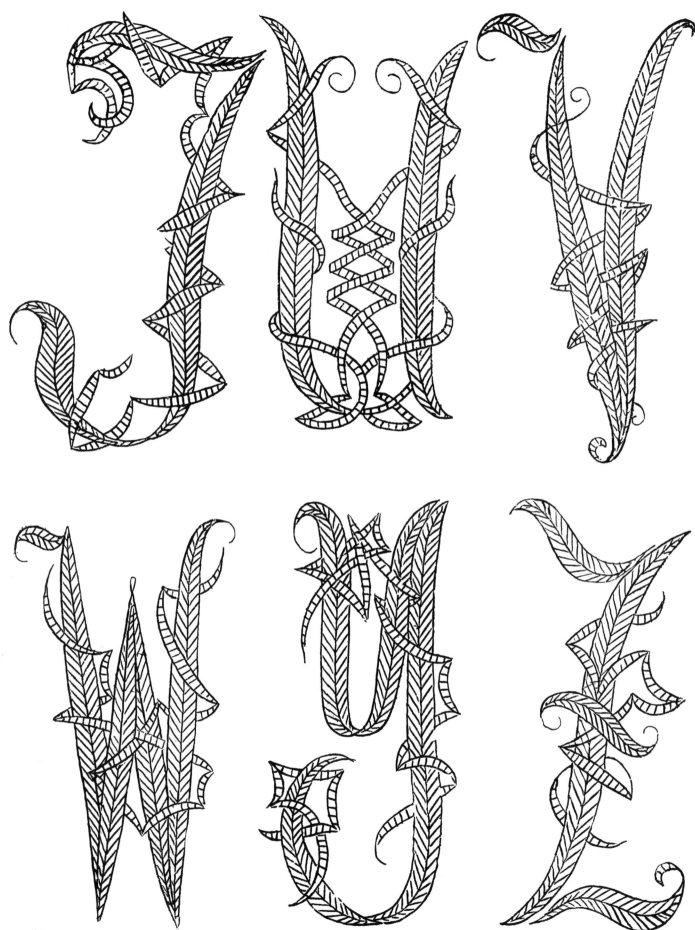

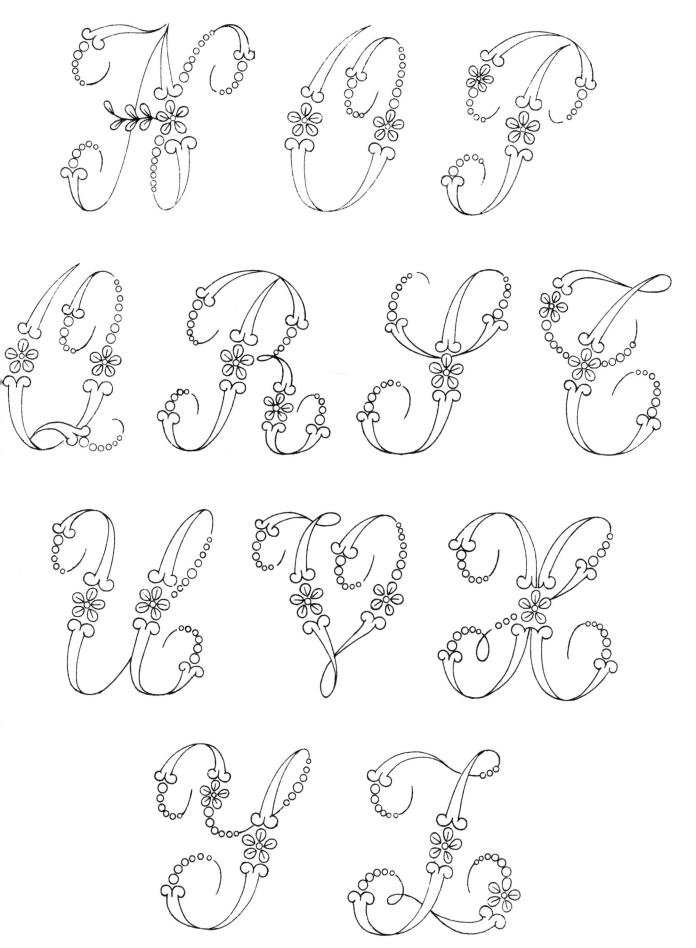

A B C D E
F G H I K
L M N O
P Q R S T
U V X Y Z

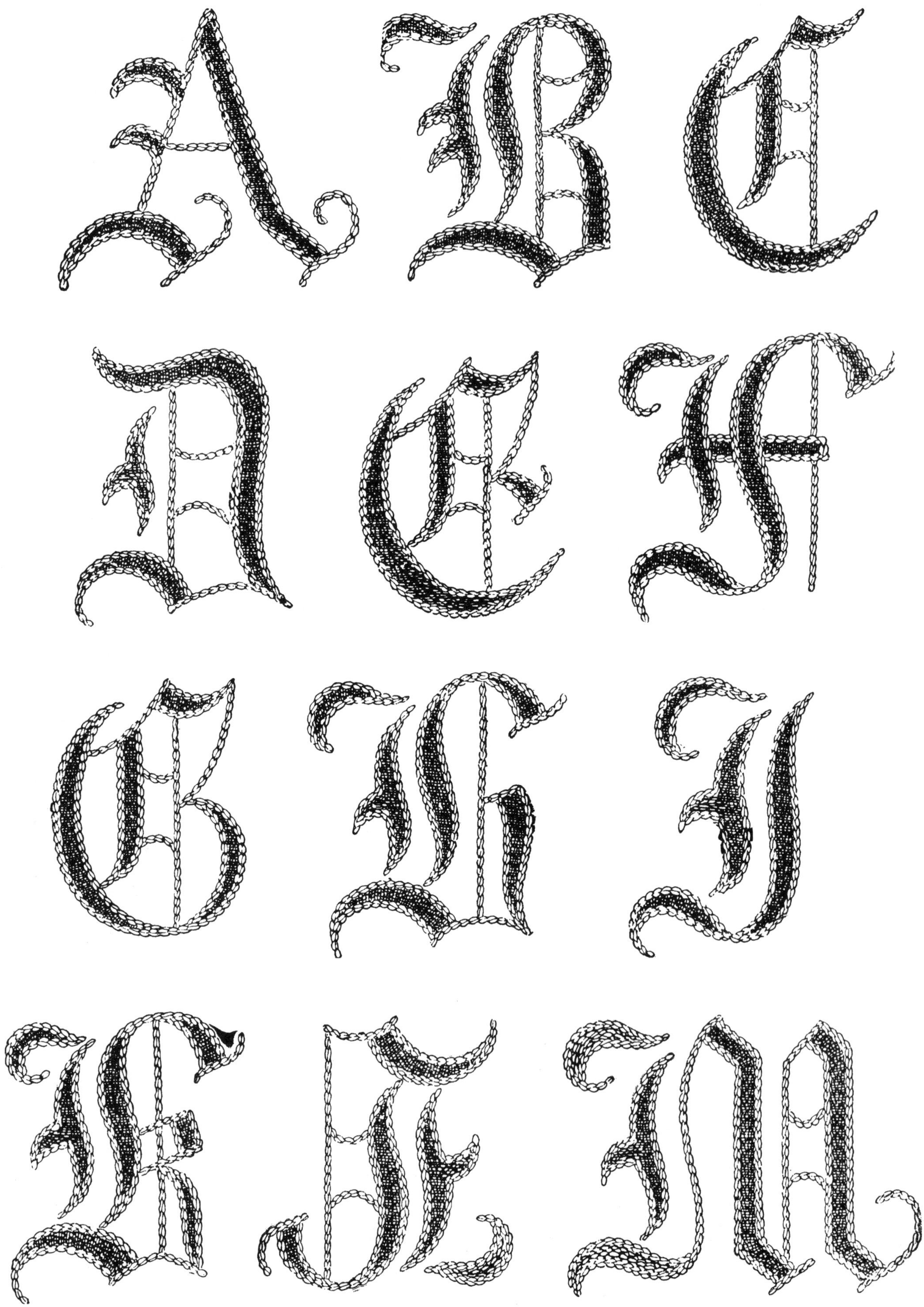

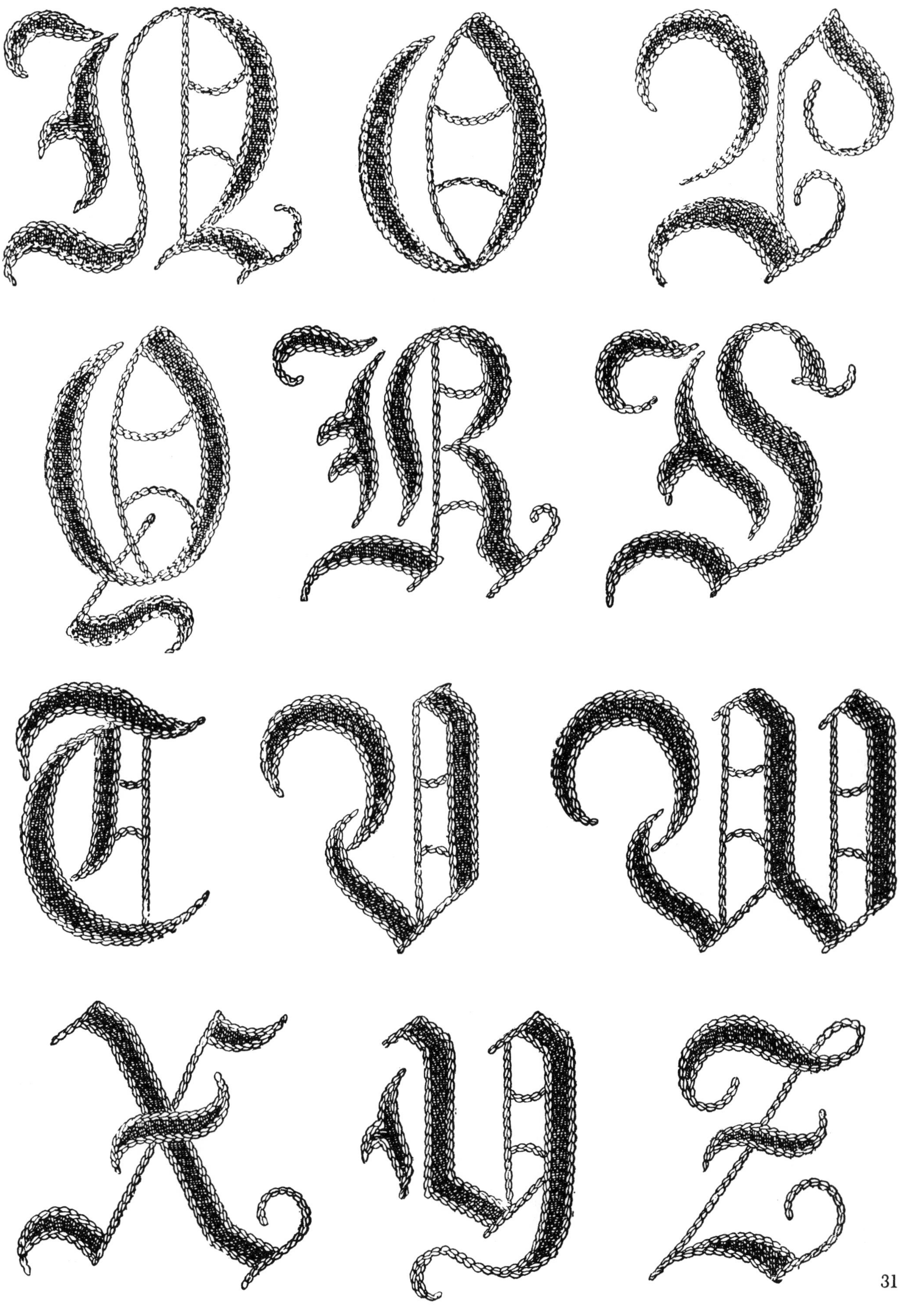

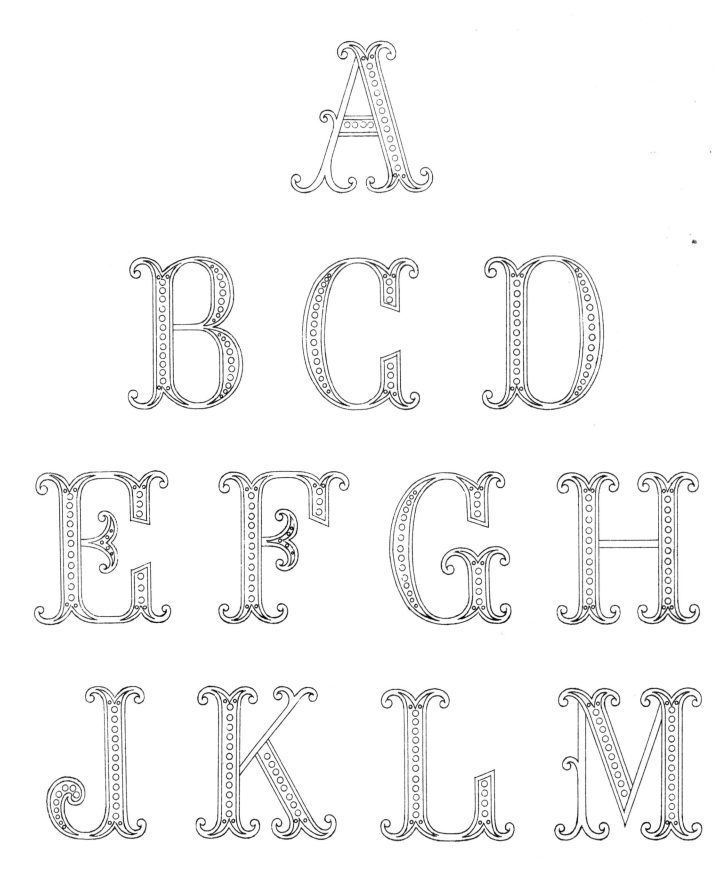

N O P Q

R S T U

V X Y

Z

A B C

D E F G

H I J

K L M

N O P
R S T U
V W X
Y Z

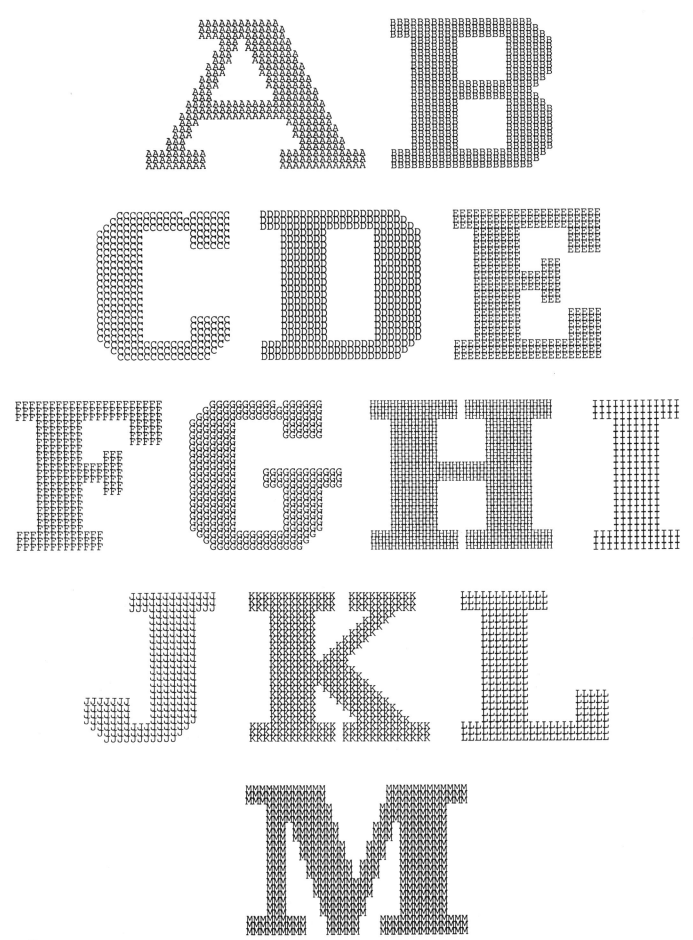

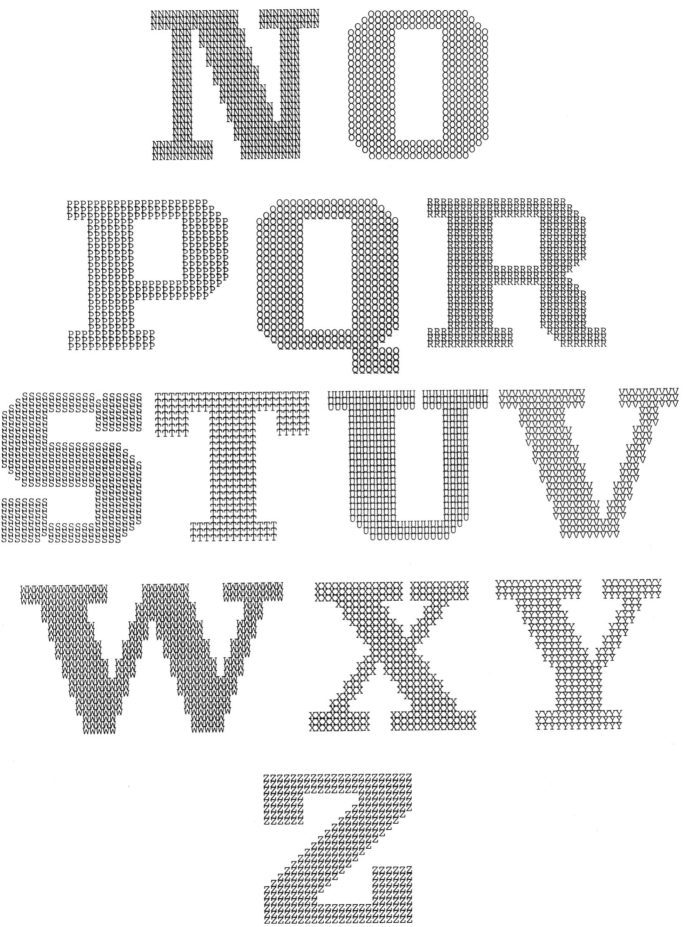

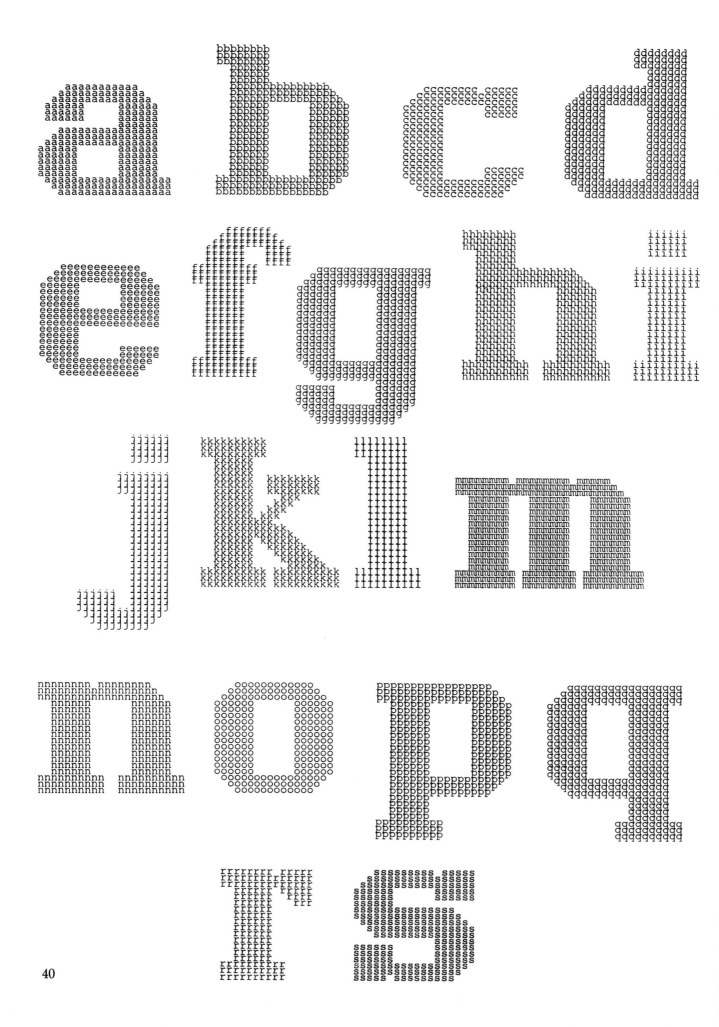

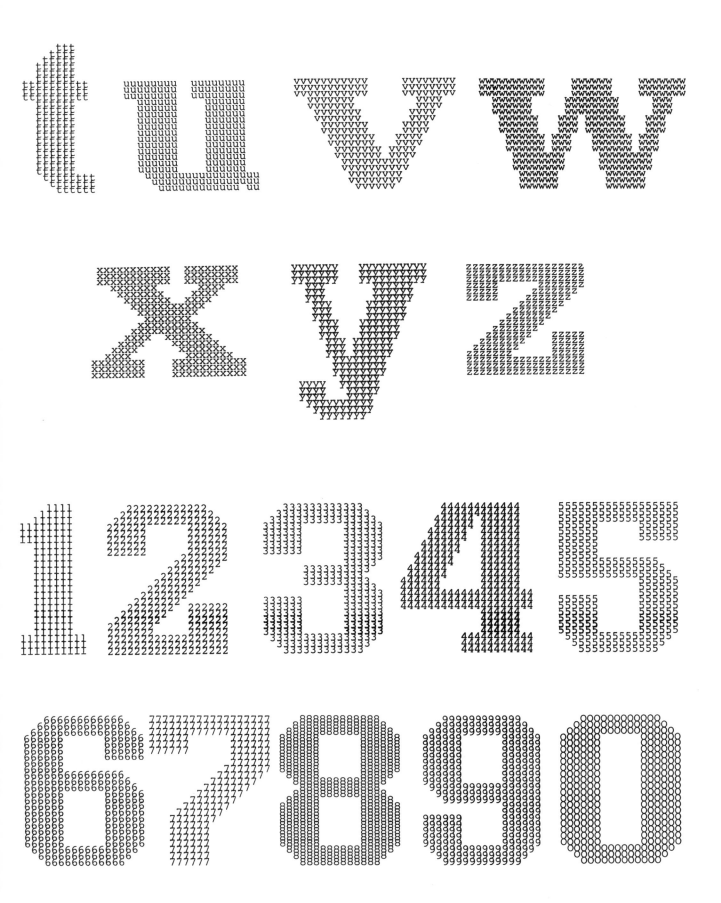

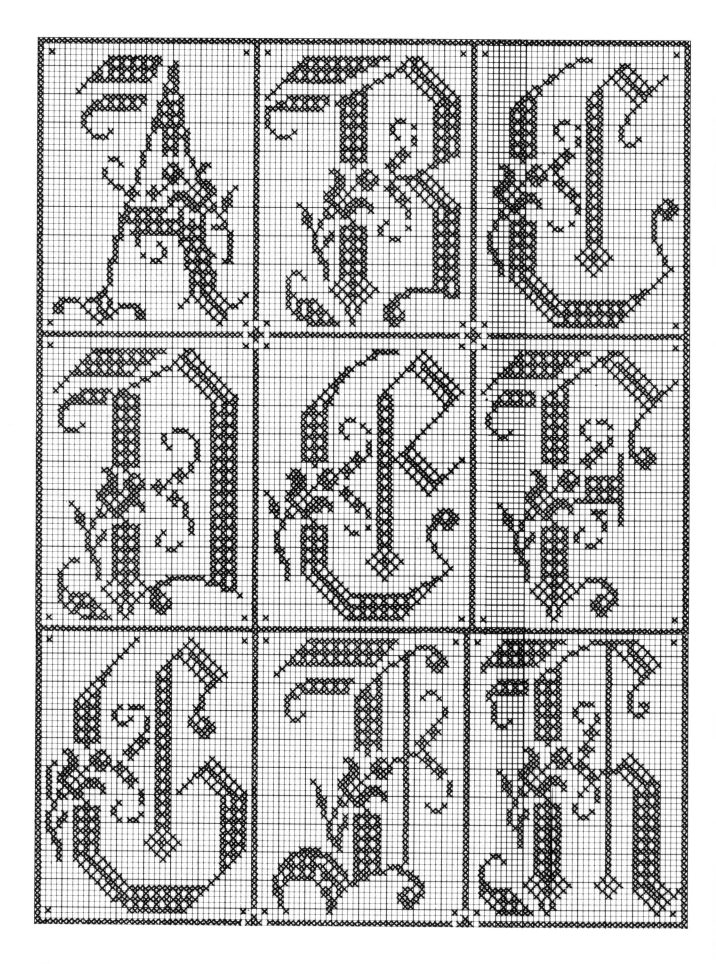

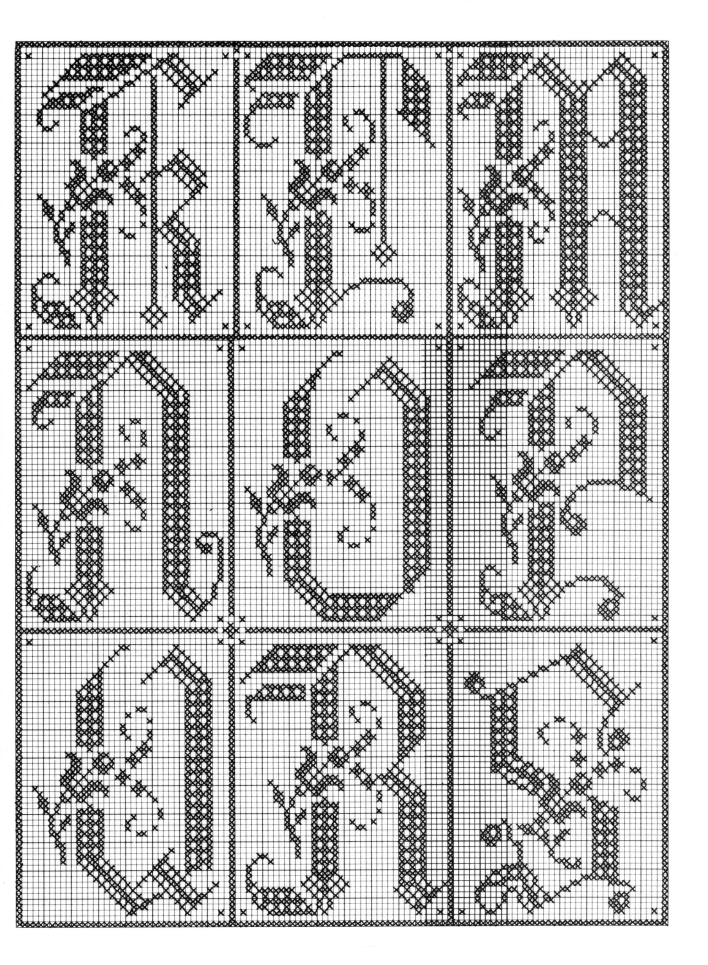

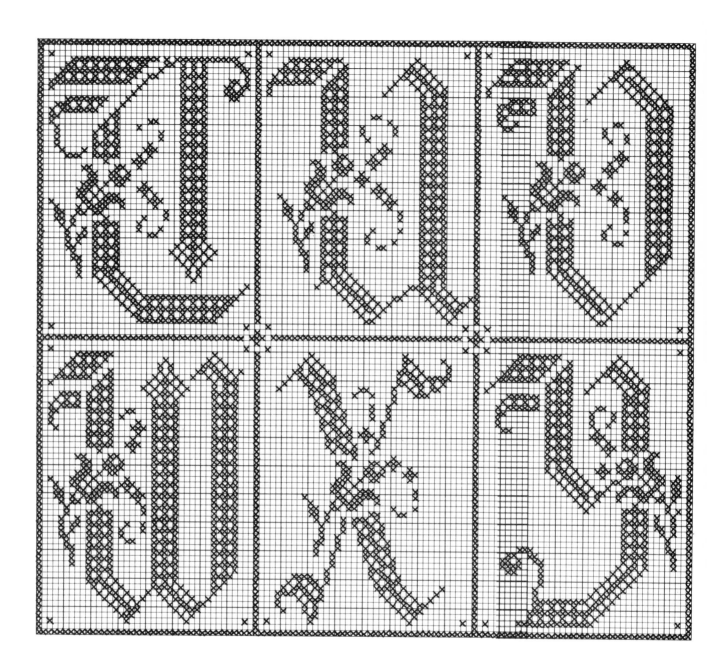

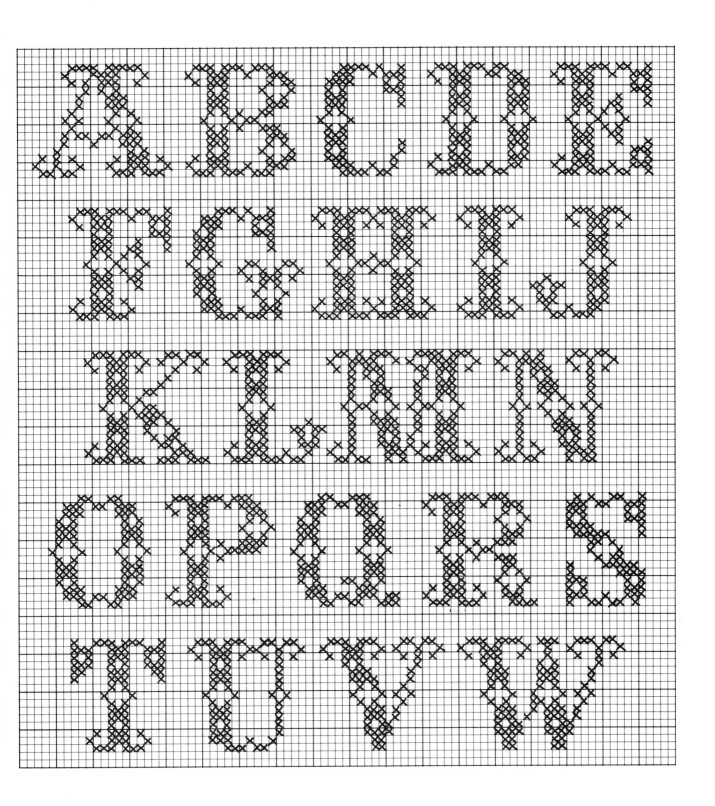

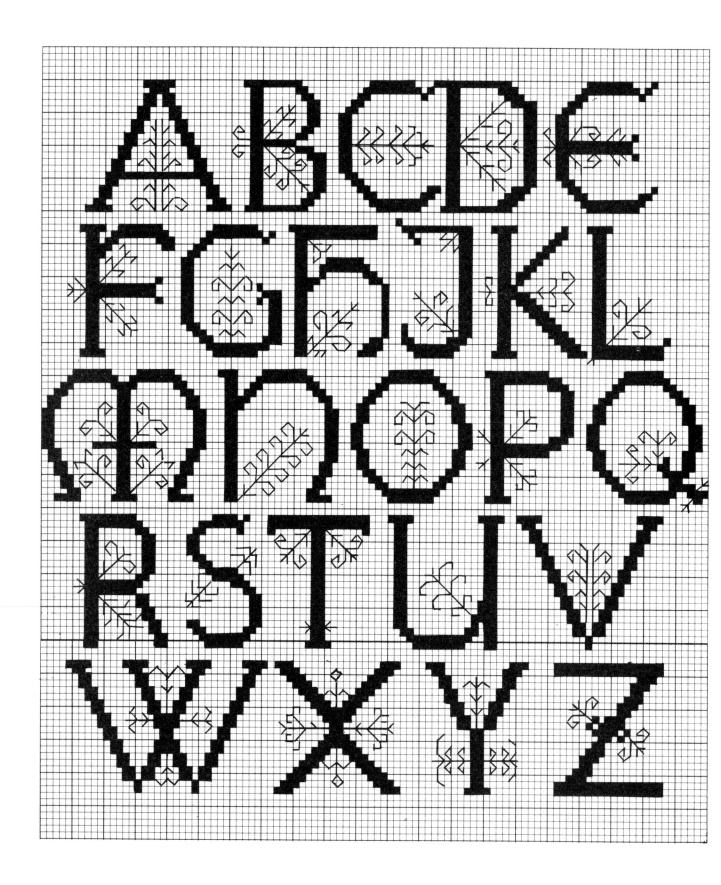

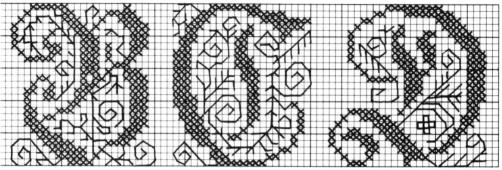

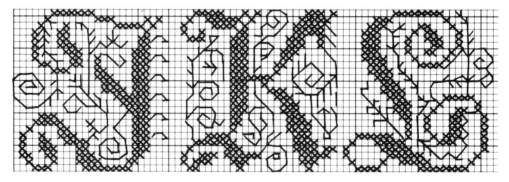

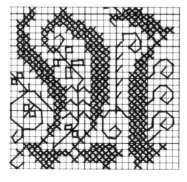

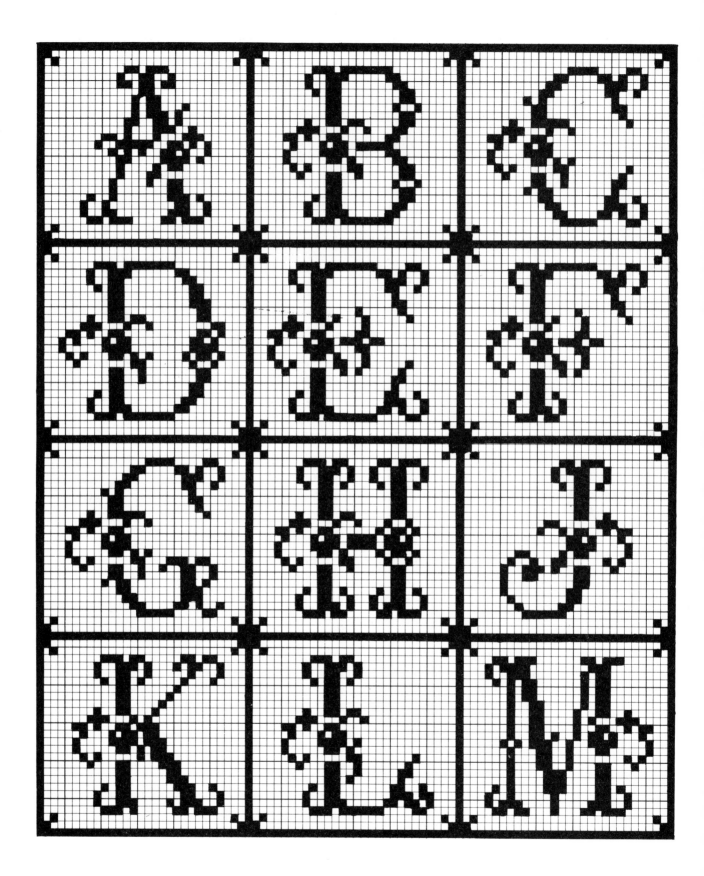

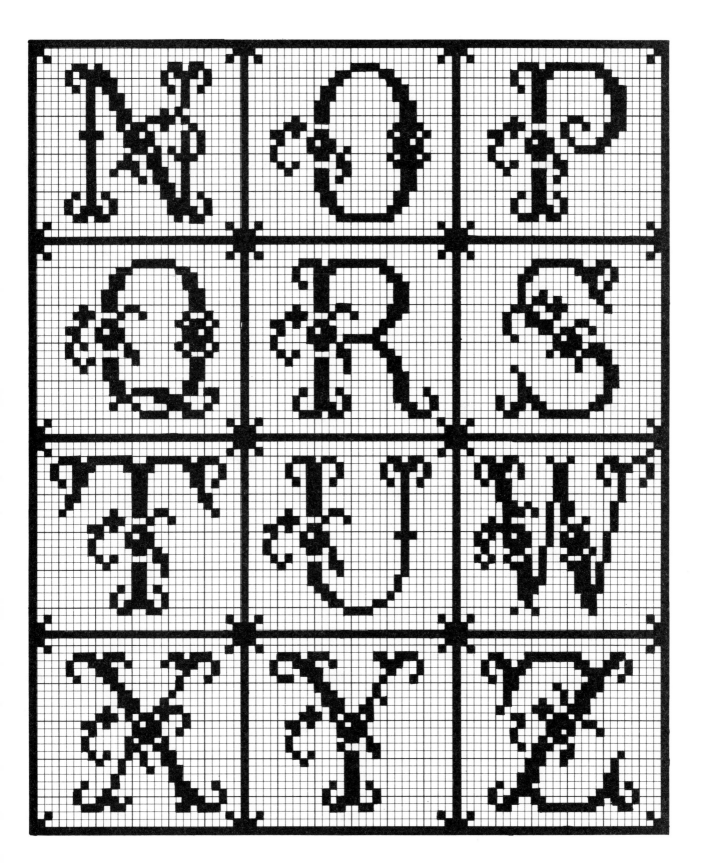

A B C D E F
G H I J K L M
N O P Q R S T
U V W X Y Z

a b c d e f g h i j k l m n

o p q r s t u v w x y z

ABCD

EFGHIL

MNOP

QRST

VXYZ

abcde

fghilmn

opqrstv

uxyz

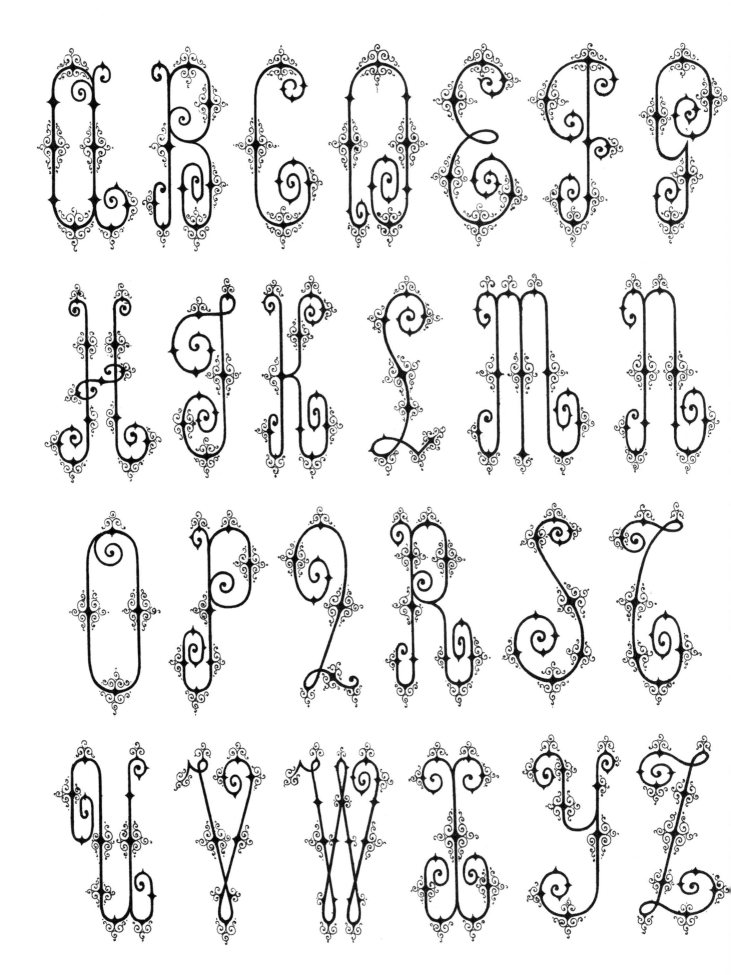

60

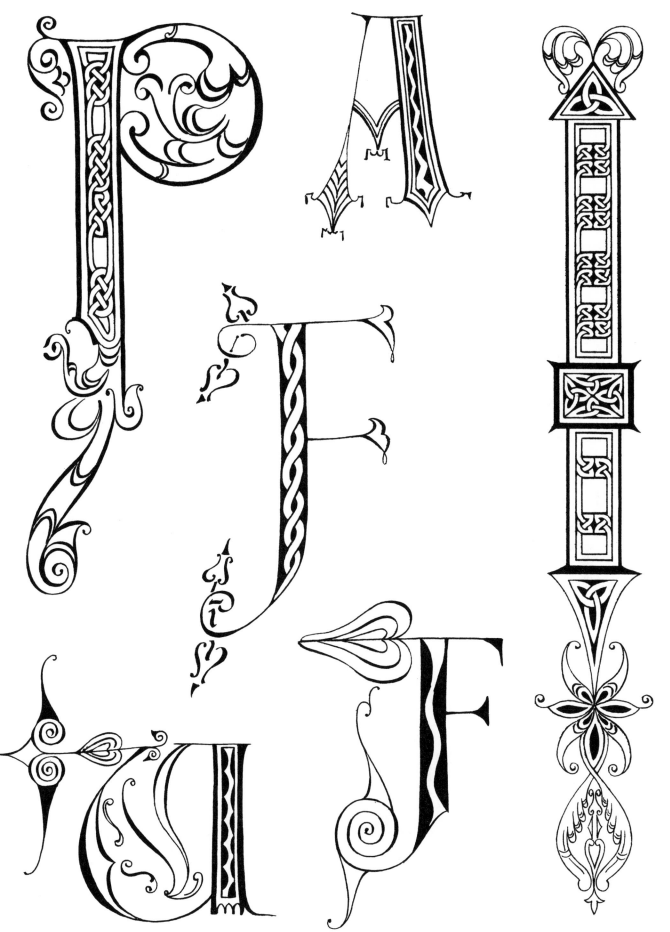

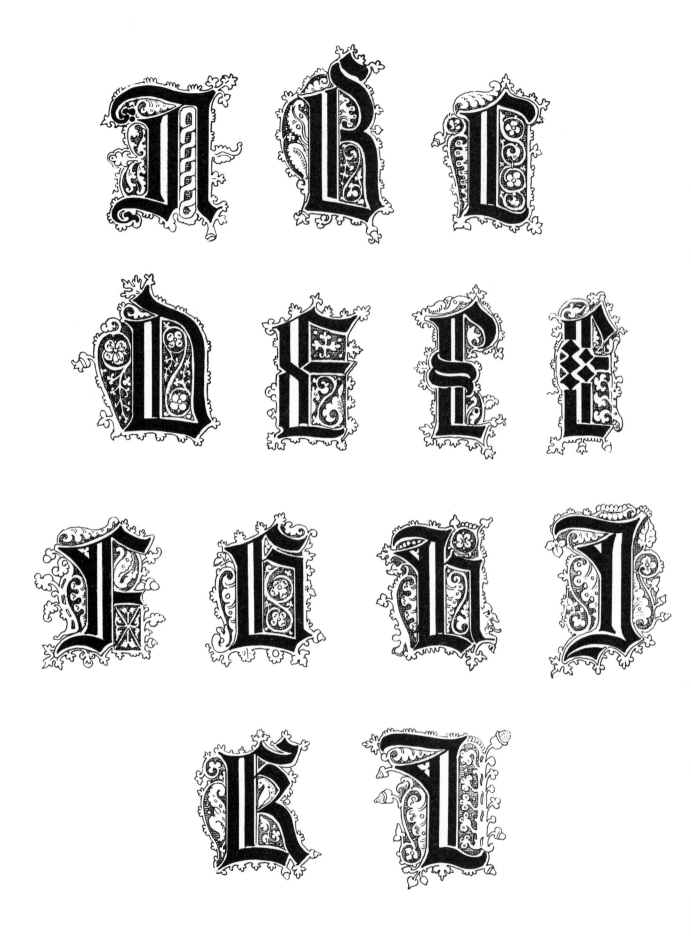

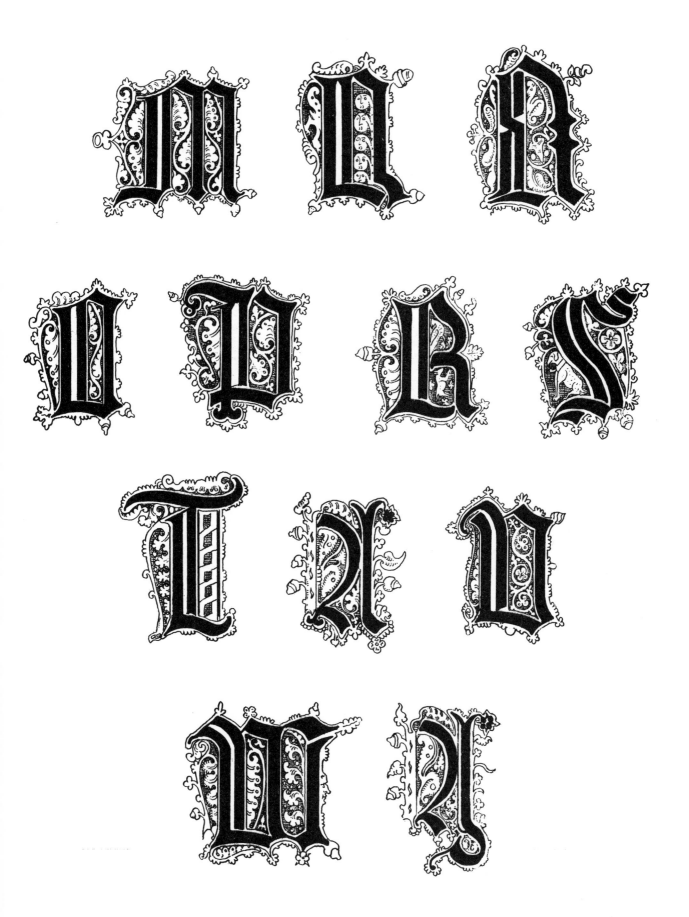

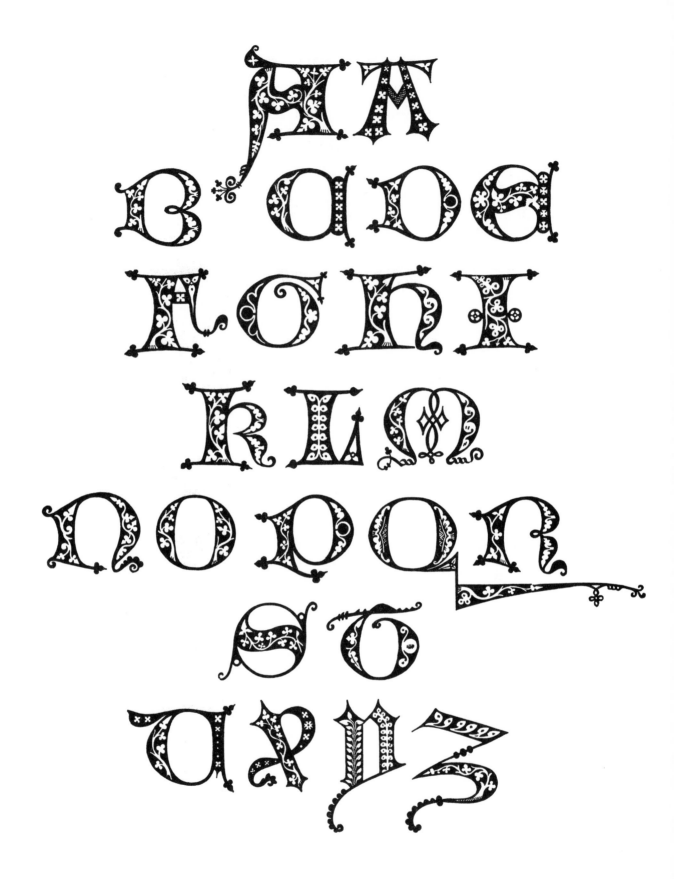

AA

BCCODE

FGBIJK

LMNHO

PQORSSS

TUVW

XXYY

2

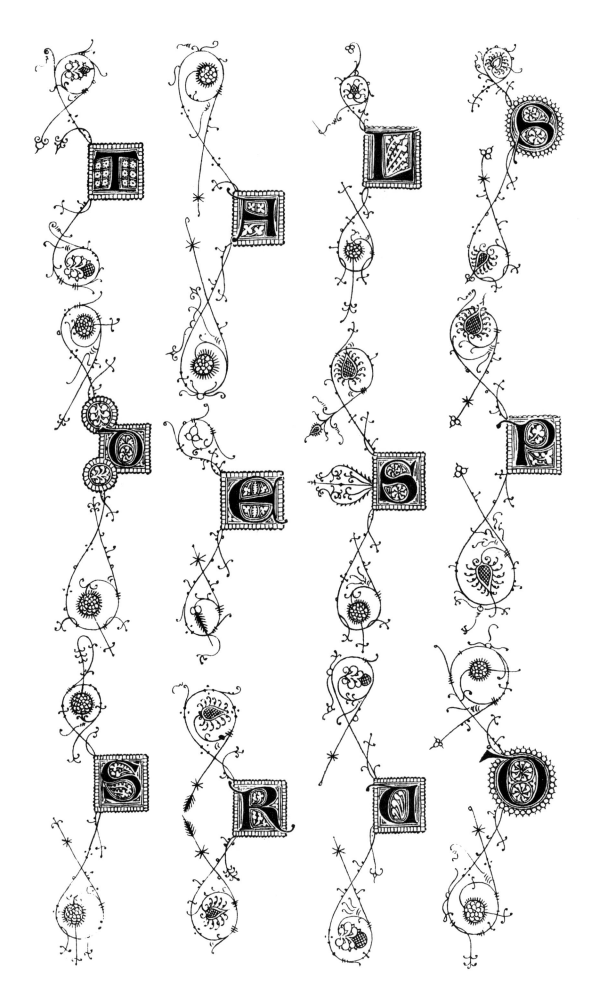

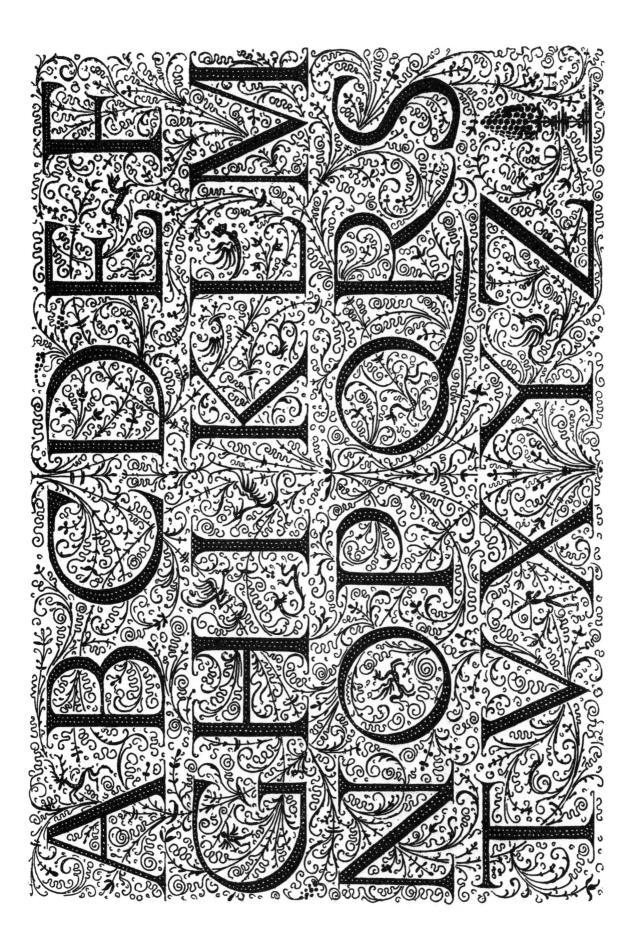

71

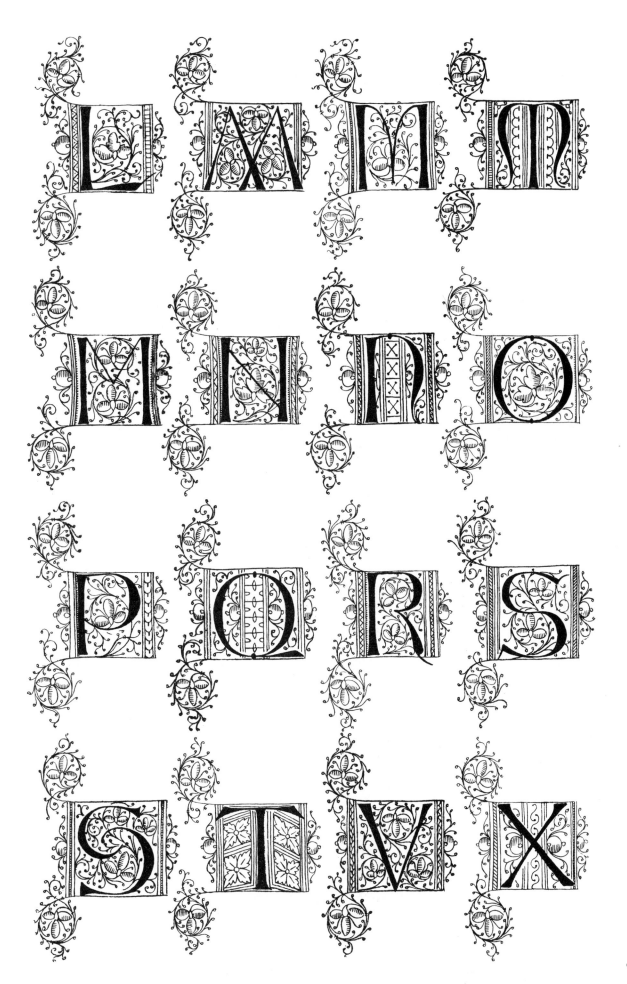

ABC
DEFGHIJK
LMNOPQR
STUVWYZ

ABC
DEFGH
IJKLMNOPQR
STUVWXYH

ABC
DEFGH
JKLMNO
PQRST
UVW
XYZ

ABCD
EFGHI
KLMNO
PQR
STV X
YZ

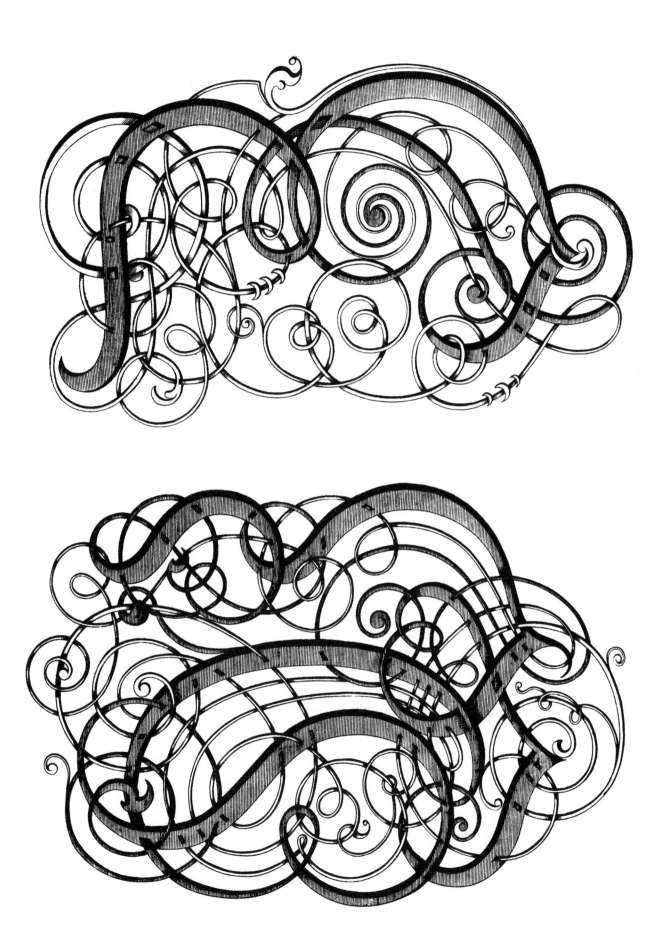

abcdefghi
lmnopqrstvu
xyz

abcdefghi
lmnopqrstv
uxyz

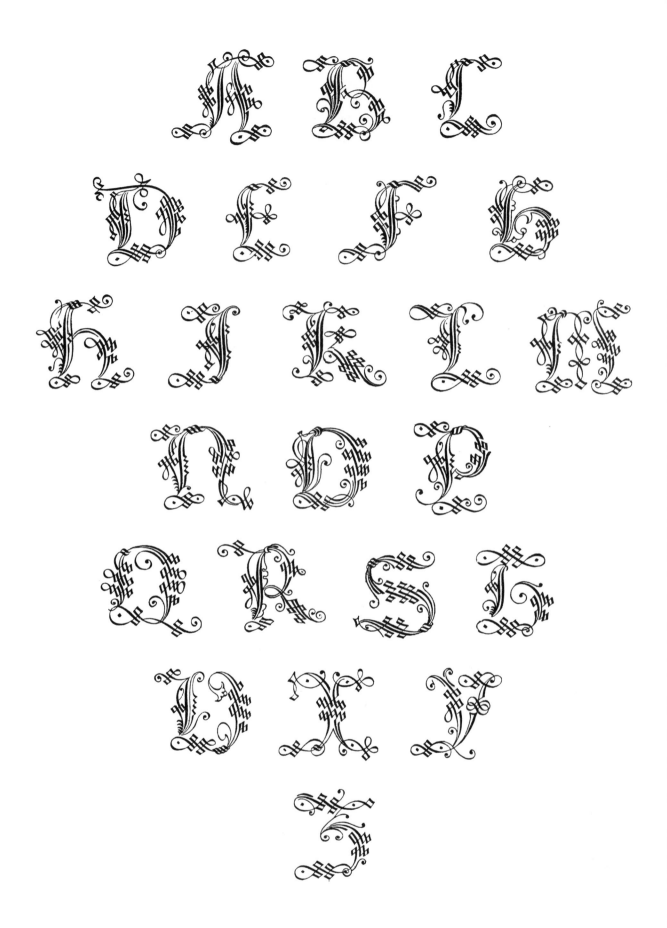

abcdeefg
hijklmmnop
qrsstuvwxyz

— 1234567890 —

ABCCDEEFCGH
IJKLCMNOPQRS
STGUVWXYZ

ABC
DEFGH
IKLMNO
PQRSTUV
WXYZ

abcdefghijklmn
opqrstuvwxyz
1234567890

A

B C D

E F G H I

K L M N O P R

S T U V W

X Y Z

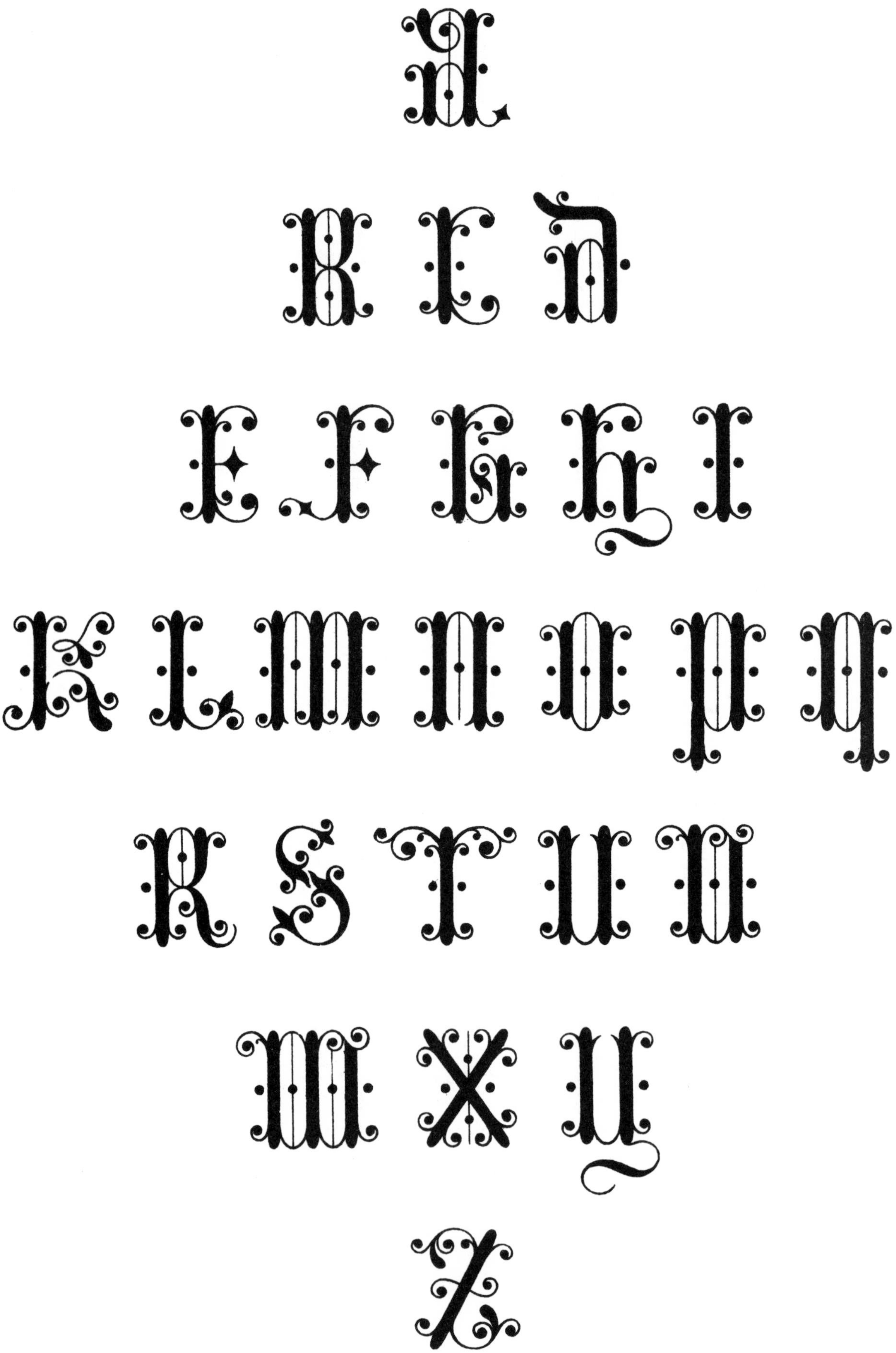

A

B C D

E F G H I J

K L M N O P Q

R S T U V

W X Y

Z

A B C D E F

G H I J K L M N O P Q

R S T U V W X Y Z ?

A B

C D & F G H

I J K L M N

O P Q R S T

U V W X Y Z

A B C D
E F G H I
J K L M N O
P Q R
S T U V W
X Y
Z

ABC
DEFGH
IJKLMN
OPQRST
UVWXYZ
&
abcdefghijklmnopqrstuvwxyz
1234567890

A B C

D E F G H I

J K L

M N O P

Q R S T U

V W Y Z

ABC
DEFG
HIJKLM
NOPQRST
UVWX
YZ

ABC
DEFGHI
JKL
MNOPQ
RSTUV
WXYZ
&

ABC
DEFGHIJK
LMN
OPQRSTU
VWXYZ
1234
567890

A
B C D
E F G H
I J K L M
N O P Q R
S T U V
W X Y
Z

A

BCD

EFGH

IJKLM

NOPQR

STUV

WXY

Z&

A B C
D E F G H I
K L L
M N O P Q R S
T U V
W X Y Z 3

ABC
DEFGHI
KLM
MNOPQRS
TUV
WXYZ

abcdef
ghiklnmopqr
stuvwxyz

abcdef
ghijklmnopqrſ
sktuvwxyz

A B C

D E E F F G H

I J K L M N

O P Q R S

T U V W X

Y Z

A

B C D

E F G h I

J K L M N

O P Q R

S T U V W

X Y Z

116

ABC
DEFG
HIJKL
MNOPQR
STUV
WXY
Z

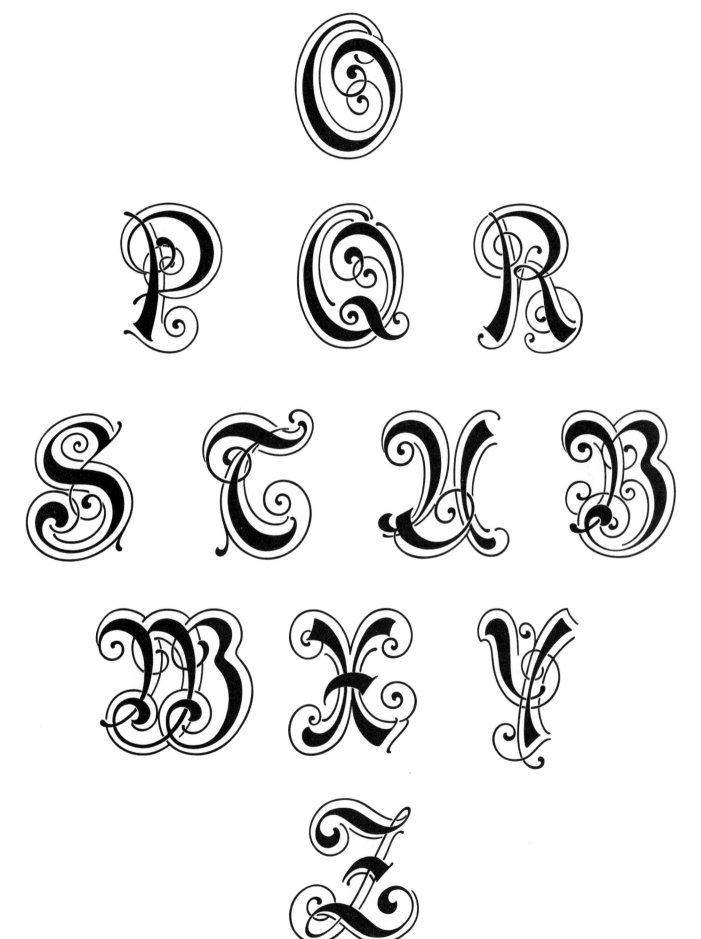

Aa Bb Cg Dd

Ee Ff Gg Hh Ii

Jj Kk Ll Mm

Nn Oo Pp Qq

Rr Ss Tt Uu Vv

Ww Xx Yy Zz